FIRENZE
MVSEI

Museum
of San Marco

Magnolia Scudieri
Museum director

GIUNTI

Graphic design: Franco Bulletti
Cover design: Laura Belforte and Fabio Filippi

Editorial manager: Claudio Pescio
Editing: Augusta Tosone

Translation: Ailsa Wood for Lexis, Florence

Photographic credits: San Marco Museum /Giunti Archives
and Foto Rabatti-Domingie, Florence

© 1999 Ministry of Artistic and Environmental Heritage –
Superintendence for Artistic and Historical Patrimony
for the districts of Florence, Pistoia and Prato
Reproduction in any form of the material in this book is prohibited.

Editorial production by Giunti Gruppo Editoriale, Florence
ISBN 88-09-01341-7

CONTENTS

BEATO ANGELICO, *Annunciation*
(detail of *Door of Silverware Cupboard*)

ENOUGH BOOKS have been written about the public museums in Florence run by the Fine Arts and Historic Works Commission to fill a large library. This is hardly surprising when one considers that the artistic heritage preserved in our museums has been famous throughout the world for centuries. For hundreds of years writers, scholars and travellers of every nationality and country have been attempting to describe all that the Florentine museums contain. They have made great efforts to explain why these museums are so fascinating, and to lead a path through paintings and sculptures for both the uninformed but willing visitor and the refined and jaded intellectual.

Over time, however, the museums have altered their aspect and their layout, the exhibitions have been arranged in new ways, the collections have been enriched (or impoverished). Attributions of works in the museums have also changed, restorations have transformed the appearance of many pieces, the rise and fall of aesthetic tendencies have led to reorganisation and the exhibition of differing works. All these things are constantly taking place within the public collections because museology and the history of art, like any intellectual endeavour, are in a constant state of progress and transformation. This explains why the literature surrounding the Florentine museums (like that of any of the world's great art collections) is so immense, and in a process of continual updating and change.

The perfect, definitive guide to a museum, any museum, does not and cannot exist.

The premise seems obvious, but is nonetheless necessary in order to understand the point of the publication introduced by these lines. From the moment when, in accordance with the application of the Ronchey law 4/93, the Giunti publishing house group took over the running of the support services within the Florentine museum system, it was decided to start at once on a standardised series of illustrated guides. These guides, displaying the cuneiform flower of "Firenze Musei" on the cover, guarantee that at the year of publication the state of each museum is exactly that described in the guide.

Certain things are obviously necessary if a museum guide is to aspire to reliability, official standing and at the same time enjoy a wide distribution: accuracy of information, high quality reproductions, an easily manageable format, a reasonable cost and – not least – a clearly written text (without, naturally, being banal or lacking in precision). Readers will judge for themselves if the guide which follows this introduction reaches these standards. I have no doubt that this will be a serious and committed judgement, just as myself and the Publisher of this guide have been serious and committed in attempting to meet the cultural needs of whoever visits our museums in the best way and with every possible care.

*Head of the Fine Arts
and Historic Works Commission
of Florence, Pistoia and Prato
(Antonio Paolucci)*

Sant'Antonino's cell no. 31
(on the wall, *Christ in Limbo*, fresco by Beato Angelico)

SAN MARCO MUSEUM

THE INITIAL STRONG IMPRESSION as you cross the threshold of the San Marco Museum is made by the setting itself, the space enclosed in the design of the rooms. This impression is balanced by that of the artistic masterpieces inside and the Museum is thus a monumental place first, and an art gallery second; it is a place of memories, Dominican memories of the illustrious members of the Order, from Sant'Antonino to Fra Angelico, from Fra Girolamo Savonarola to Fra Bartolomeo, not to mention the famous figures who lived in the monastery, and other artists such as Fra Paolino, and Marco and Francesco della Robbia. Another decisive factor adding to the building's charm and importance is the fact that its appearance and spiritual atmosphere have remained unchanged over the centuries, despite the various layers of historical events.

The Museum is situated in the oldest part of the monastery occupying about half the total space. The building has expanded over time, now taking up a whole block, and part of it is still occupied by friars today. The oldest section of the building, built over the medieval Sylvestrian monastery, was constructed by the architect Michelozzo at the specific request of Cosimo il Vecchio de' Medici and at his expense, to house the reformed Dominicans of Fiesole, an order at that time led by Antonino Pierozzi. Over about ten years (1436-1446) Michelozzo completed an extremely modern and functional monasterial building project (considered to be at the avantgarde of its kind) which contributed to the glorification of Medicean patronage. Michelozzo made use of the pre-existent wall structures of the Sylvestrian monastery complex, now in ruins, which date back to the end of the 13th century. Recently discovered painting in the dormitory area (1992) indicates that the perimeter walls of the Hospice (on Piazza San Marco) and those of the Large Refectory (on via La Pira) belong to the late 13th or early 14th century building. Michelozzo ably linked together the ground floor rooms around a harmoniously-proportioned cloister and raised the levels of these buildings to create the dormitories on the first floor with a large number of cells to suit an expanding monastery. The result is an enormous complex, rationally organized in well-articulated spaces, fulfilling all the most modern requirements of a large monastic community whose specific functions were denoted by symbolic images frescoed above the entrance doors by Fra Giovanni da Fiesole, known as Beato Angelico, one of the most important painters of the Renaissance. The task of frescoing the entire monastery, from the cloisters to the cells, with images for group and personal meditation was entrusted to him as a well-known and admired painter.

A visit to the Museum begins on the ground floor, at the cloister known as the Sant'Antonino Cloister, named after the first prior of the monastery who was later Archbishop of Florence from 1446 and canonized in 1523. The frescoes depicting scenes from the life of Sant'Antonino are painted

Sant'Antonino Cloister

in 28 lunettes by the most fashionable 17th century historical painters. The cloister, bounded by the clean façades of the dormitories, punctuated by the small mullioned windows of the cells, offers a simple architectural view of harmonious colours and proportions. While Fra Angelico's splendid fresco of *St. Dominic worships the Crucifix* (sum-

marising the Dominicans' continuing dialogue with the Crucifix) stands out opposite the entrance, the visitor's route leads away to the right alongside the entrance to the large room still known as the Hospice, in accordance with its allotted function as a reception room. This function is recalled in a lunette by Fra Angelico above the door depicting

Christ the pilgrim welcomed by the Dominicans. Since 1921 all Beato Angelico's panel paintings have been on display here, having been gathered together from churches and monasteries in and around Florence; the paintings came into State possession following the suppression of religious institutions in the 18th and 19th centuries.

The cloister also leads to a wing of the building originally used as the friars' refectory and today largely dedicated to the collection of 16th century works by Fra Bartolomeo and the "San Marco School", which sprang up around him and was diffused in the early decades of the sixteenth century. Also in this wing are the Washroom, the Large Refectory, the kitchen and its annexes – today known as the Fra Bartolomeo room and the Standard room, whose name derives from the large 16th century banner depicting *Sant'Antonino worships the Crucifix*. From here the visitor continues towards the small "Spesa" (or Shopping) Cloister, so-called because it was equipped for the purchase of consumer goods. The cloister gave access to the service area from the lodge, before reaching the large vegetable gardens to the rear.

From the Sant'Antonino Cloister a door to the right leads to the Chapterhouse, on whose end wall Fra Angelico has left us a spectacular *Crucifixion* with all the founding saints of the Monastic Orders and the Dominican family tree. A hallway connects the Sant'Antonino Cloister to the larger and slightly later St.Dominic Cloister. This was completed in the 16th century and illustrated at the end of the 18th by Alessandro Gherardini and his co-workers, with *Scenes from the life of St. Dominic*, whose statue is placed at the centre. In the north-west corner is the entrance to the former apothecary which was until recently still functional. The cloister, its appearance drastically altered by modifications, belongs to the friars and is not part of the Museum.

The hall also leads to the staircase up to the first floor dormitories, where the famous cycle of frescoes painted by Beato Angelico and his assistants can be seen in the 43 cells built before 1443 (the year in which pope Eugenio IV consecrated the new church and monastery). This is one of the largest Renaissance cycles in existence combining spirituality and realism, reality and unreality, in a new language which transformed the cultural heritage of the past without renouncing it. Now, as then, the austere but serene appearance of the rooms is evocative of the monastery's meditative atmosphere, where life was divided into precise prayer and study duties far from the clamour of city life. At the end of the Novices' Corridor are the chapel and Savonarola's cells, where the mortal remains and belongings of the famous monk are preserved. This area recalls the tragic moments experienced by the city during the preaching and punishment of the friar from Ferrara.

On the same floor, but on the opposite side, is a room designed with great architectural expertise: the huge Library, designed by Michelozzo as a three-nave basilica, once contained many precious Latin and Greek manuscripts. In the 19th century, after the suppressions,

these were transferred to the large public libraries, the Medicea Lau-
renziana and the National Central. In the Library, annexed to the
Greek Room with its beautiful 15th century wooden ceiling, some of
the more than one hundred illuminated choir-books in the Museum
are on display.

Returning to the ground floor, we complete the visit to the north wing
including the Small Refectory (frescoed by Domenico Ghirlandaio around
1480 with a *Last Supper* which is copied in Ognissanti), the Lodge (con-
sisting of a long gallery with several adjoining rooms used as an infirmary after the 17th century), the Barn Courtyard and the small 14th century Sylvestrian Cloister, which can both be visited in spring and summer. All these rooms contain a particular section of the Museum dedicated to Ancient Florence, including a collection of stone, wooden and
pictorial findings from buildings and churches in the old city centre, demolished from 1881 onwards when a radical restoration project for the
city was put into effect. Part of the collection is situated in the area un-
derneath the monastery (visits by appointment) where all the tombstones
which until 1970 occupied the walls of the Sant'Antonino Cloister are
kept. This section, prior to that devoted to Beato Angelico, was one of the
first to be put together in the history of the San Marco Museum and was
undertaken in 1869 with the aim of improving the Museum's general appearance, not only through Fra Angelico's cycle of frescoes, until then
forbidden to the public, but also through the famous figures connected
with the monastery such as Girolamo Savonarola, Sant'Antonino, Fra
Bartolomeo and Cosimo de' Medici. The fulfilment of the cherished dream
– the creation of a monographical Beato Angelico Museum – was only to
take place in 1921, when the San Marco Museum had already taken shape
and been divided into different sections.

In the last twenty years the Museum administration has tried to en-
hance this aspect along with the others, beginning with the restoration of all Beato Angelico's frescoes and Ghirlandaio's *Last Supper*, to
allow visitors to fully perceive the history and meaning of the whole
Museum complex and, through the setting and history of works collected there, to better understand the city's evolution.

SANT'ANTONINO CLOISTER

The visitor enters the cloister, built by Michelozzo in about 1440, through a narrow hallway with 18th and 19th century sepulchral monuments and tomb-stones which bear witness to the old custom of burying the dead in the spaces alongside the church. The cloister is behind the church and overlooked by a large cedar planted in the last century, and it introduces the visitor to the sight of the splendidly poised architecture of the monastery, a typical example of measured and orderly Florentine Renaissance architecture. The gallery rests on five columns per side, decorated with elegant ionic capitals with low arches marking the area with a rhythm proportionate with human dimensions, which suggest a secluded space echoed by the small single-mullioned windows on the first floor, each indicating a friar's cell. This simplicity and reciprocity can also be found in the colours of the principal materials used: white lime, grey stone, red brick. The sight of St. Dominic worships the Crucifix, *painted by Beato Angelico opposite the entrance is uplifting. Originally this was the only painted image (apart from five little lunettes above the door) decorating the white cloister. The* Scenes from the life of Sant'Antonino *cycle and the other frescoes now occupying 28 lunettes along the walls were painted during the 17th century.*

BERNARDINO POCCETTI
Sant'Antonino is made Archbishop of Florence

1608-1609
Fresco, 230×412

This is an important scene in the cycle painted, with a great deal of help, by Poccetti, the "great historical fresco painter" between 1602 and 1612, but only completed in 1693 by Pier Dandini. The cycle is dedicated to Antonino Pierozzi, first prior of the monastery and later bishop of Florence (1446-1455), canonised in 1523. The elements of particular value in the fresco are the façade of the cathedral prior to its demolition in 1587, and the insertion of Savonarola on the right, which is completely anachronistic but of great symbolic importance, as it demonstrates the vitality of Fra Girolamo's worship and its idealised link to Sant'Antonino.

BEATO ANGELICO
St. Dominic worships the Crucifix

c. 1442
Fresco, 340×206

CECCO BRAVO
The Mourners

1628
Detached frescoes
413×86 each

Fra Angelico's beautiful fresco symbolises the dialogue of St. Dominic (and therefore the Order) with the Crucifix, and his devotion to it. In the seventeenth century, when the Fabbroni family came into possession of that side of the Cloister and made it a family burial vault, the fresco was set in a marble frame and flanked by the mourning figures, now darkened with time and by the fixatives applied over the years. Despite this alteration, the emotional impact of the image is still undamaged in the absolute synthesis between the Saint's expressive realism, explored by the light in every crease of his face, and his soul, and the symbolic abstraction of the scene outside real space and time.

13

Pilgrims' Hospice

This large room, which can be entered from the right side of the cloister, occupies all the part of the building facing onto Piazza San Marco and already existed in the Middle Ages when the monastery was inhabited by the Sylvestrian monks. On the perimeter walls, high up right under the roof, are traces of pictorial decorations, some dating back to the 14th century. When the monastery was rebuilt in the 15th century the architect covered the whole area with cross vaults and raised the building to build the second friars' dormitory. Inside, probably subdivided, there was also a pilgrims' hospice, which can be deduced from the image painted by Fra Angelico on one of the doors showing Christ the pilgrim welcomed by the Dominicans. Today it is the home of almost all the panel paintings by Fra Angelico, collected from the churches and convents of Florence and crowded into the Florentine Galleries after the suppression of the monasteries in the 19th century.

Beato Angelico
Triptych of St. Peter the Martyr

before 1429

Panel
137×168
Inv. 1890, no. 8769

Mentioned prior to 1429, the triptych represents a stage of his early work, under the influence of Gentile da Fabriano and Masaccio. The shape of the panel, the alternate use of gold and blue in the backgrounds and the twisted figures record a transitional phase from the late Gothic to the Renaissance schemes, which only in the next decade would lead to the realization of a new scheme of *Holy Conversation* in a square panel with figures in a semicircle.

BEATO ANGELICO
Deposition
LORENZO MONACO.
"Noli me tangere", The
Resurrection, and
Pious Women at the Tomb
(in the cusps)
St. Onophrius' and St.
Nicholas' stories
(in the predella panels)

1425-1432
Panel
185×176
Inv. 1890, no. 8509

Commissioned from
Lorenzo Monaco by
Palla Strozzi, a cultured
banker rival of the Medi-
ci, for the altar of the Holy Trinity church sacri-
sty, this Altarpiece was
destined for his father
Nofri's mortuary chapel.
Before his death in 1425,
the painter only man-
aged to paint the cusps
and the predella in typ-
ical late Gothic style. The
task of completing the
altarpiece was entrusted
to Fra Angelico, who
painted the central part
and the newels by 1432.
This painting is perhaps
Fra Angelico's greatest
panel painting and in-
dicates the turning point
in a modern direction of
the artist's activity, and
consequently of the who-
le of Florentine art.
The free spatial loca-
tion, both open and se-
vere, the new realistic
attention to nature, landscape, physiognomy and
emotions all make it one
of the first real Renais-
sance paintings.
The figure with black
headpiece may be Mi-
chelozzo; Palla Strozzi
is the figure holding the
nails and crown of thorns
and his son Lorenzo is
the kneeling figure.

15

BEATO ANGELICO
Marriage of the Virgin
(above)
Funeral of the Virgin
(below)

1430-1435
Predella panels
19×50, 19×51
Inv. 1890, nos. 1493, 1501

These two paintings made up the sections of the predella panel, now in the Uffizi Gallery, with the *Coronation of the Virgin* painted for the nun's choir in Sant'Egidio, the church annexed to the Santa Maria Nuova hospital. The proximity in style to the great *Coronation* in San

Domenico at Fiesole, today in the Louvre, leads us to date them around the early 1430's, and it is now agreed that the panel also belongs to this period.

The two paintings, drawn in a style evocative of medieval tradition, are still linked, stylistically, to Gothic culture. They are rich in chromatic and calligraphic preciosity in late Gothic taste, which is particularly evident in the drapery of the undulating silhouettes.

These show at the same time, however, perfect knowledge of the rules

of perspective and the awareness of the necessity of putting these rules into practice always and everywhere. This can be clearly seen in the devices used to suggest spatial depth within the narrow horizontal surface available: note for example the building glimpsed as a zig-zag and the perspective illusion of the candles.

The two panels therefore represent an example of the synthesis between the old and new cultures in which Beato Angelico was a Master.

BEATO ANGELICO
Last Judgement
(whole and detail)
c. 1425
Panel
105×210
Inv. 1890, no. 8505

This painting came from the Church of Santa Maria degli Angeli adjoining the old monastery of Camaldoli and was long considered to be the final part of a chorister chair backrest, dated around 1431.

Recently however both these hypotheses have been revised. The work has been dated further back, halfway through the third decade of the 15th century, just after the San Dominico of Fiesole Altarpiece and the *Thebaid* in the Uffizi. It has also been highlighted that the highly cultured significance of the composition context was perhaps developed at the suggestion of the humanist theologian Ambrogio Traversari, an expert in patristics, who may have inspired the presence next to Christ of Old Testament figures.

The painting's ingenious pyramidic composition audaciously combines the medieval scheme of the representation of Judgment through the superimposition of registers.

The idea of the tombs at the centre indicating a series in perspective is a clear declaration of full adherence to a new Renaissance language.

BEATO ANGELICO
Naming of the Baptist
c.1430
Panel
26×24
Inv. 1890, no. 1499

This small painting is part of a predella, recently almost completely rebuilt, whose other panels are in Fort Worth, Philadelphia and San Francisco.

The painting was certainly completed before 1435, when Andrea di Giusto copied it into a polyptych today contained in the Prato art gallery; however it is dated at the end of the third decade of the century. At this time the artist was still mindful of exquisite late Gothic daintiness in the changing figures and worked in a spatial and architectural setting which was strongly influenced by Masaccio and especially by the frescoes of the Cappella Brancacci. Moreover, the clean background architecture with its measured domestic proportions cannot help but recall the buildings in the style of Michelozzo, pushing the date a little further back towards the beginning of the works in San Marco.

BEATO ANGELICO
Virgin of the Star
(Virgin and Child,
the Eternal, angels) (above)
Coronation
of the Virgin (below)
Annunciation and
Adoration of the Magi
(not shown)

c.1430
Panels, 84×51, 69×37, 84×50
Inv. San Marco, nos. 274, 275

The tabernacles, perhaps originally designed as reliquaries, are part of a series, a quarter of which, with the *Funeral Rites* and *Assumption of the Virgin*, is now in Boston. They may have been commissioned by the dominican Fra Giovanni Masi, sacristan of Santa Maria Novella, who died in 1434. They were certainly completed before this date, around the 1430's, but the work was probably spread out over time due to the outstanding similarities to some large paintings dated from the beginning of the third decade to 1433.

The *Virgin of the Star* alludes to the *Tabernacle of the Linen-drapers*, the Louvre *Coronation* is the reference for the tabernacle of the same name, and the early *Missal 558* for the one with the *Annunciation* which may have been painted first.

19

**BEATO ANGELICO
AND ASSISTANTS**
*Doors of the Silverware
Cupboard*

1448-1455

Panels, 123×123, 123×44,
123×160, 123×160
Inv. 1890, nos. 8489-8491,
8510, 8492, 8500-8502

The eight panels with thirty-five scenes from the Old and New Testaments originally formed the door of a room where the ritual silverware was kept in the church of Santissima Annunziata in Florence. The work was commissioned in 1448 by Piero di Cosimo de' Medici to Fra Angelico who definitely conceived the whole cycle of scenes and personally painted at least the first nine, using assistants for the others. These included Alesso Baldovinetti and others who had already worked on the San Marco fres-

BEATO ANGELICO
*Mystical wheel with the vision of Ezekiel: Annunciation, Nativity, Circumcision,
Adoration of the Magi, Presentation in the Temple, Flight into Egypt, Massacre of
the Innocent, Jesus among the Scribes*
Panels, 123×123, Inv. 1890, nos. 8489-8491

coes. Many of the scenes, painted as accurately as if they were miniatures, recall compositions already used on a large scale, especially in the cell frescoes. Especially interesting is the constant reference to the coeval architecture, as in the *Presentation in the Temple* which shows us the inside of the apsidal part of San Marco church restored by Michelozzo at the same time as the monastery.

ALESSO BALDOVINETTI
Wedding at Cana (above),
Baptism of Christ, Transfiguration (not shown)
Panel, 123×44, Inv. 1890, no. 8510

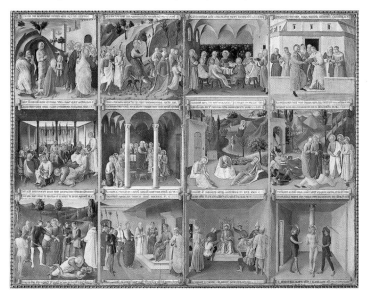

BEATO ANGELICO
Resurrection of Lazarus, Entrance in Jerusalem, Last Supper, Betrayal of Judas, Washing the feet, Institution of the Eucharist, Christ in the Garden of olives, Kiss of Judas, Christ's Capture, Christ before Caiaphas, Mocking of Christ, Christ tied to the pillar
Panels, 123×160, Inv. 1890, nos. 8492-8500

21

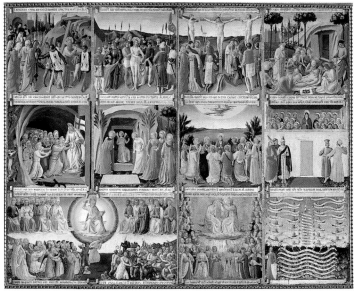

BEATO ANGELICO
The Path to Calvary, Division of the Vestments, Crucifixion, Deposition into the Tomb, Descent into Limbo, Pious Women at the Tomb, Ascension of the Virgin into Heaven, Pentecost, Final Judgment, Coronation of the Virgin and *Lex Amoris*
Panels, 123×160, Inv. 1890, nos. 8501-8502

ZANOBI STROZZI
Enthroned Virgin and Child with four angels

c. 1440
Panel, 127×110
Inv. 1890, no. 3204

This is one of the few paintings that can definitely be attributed to this painter, who worked as an assistant in the cells but was more famous for the San Marco illuminated choir-books which reveal other cultural components as well as the influence of Fra Angelico.

BEATO ANGELICO
Lamentation over
the Dead Christ

1436-1441
Panel
105×164
Inv. 1890, no. 8487

This painting is stylistically close to the fresco in Cell no. 2 in San Marco and was commissioned in 1436 by Fra Sebastiano Benintendi, a descendent of the Blessed Villana delle Botti (who died in 1360), depicted wearing nun's habit next to St. Catherine.

The painting was finished in 1441 as shown by the inscription on the Virgin's cloak and was destined for the Compagnia di Santa Maria in the church of Croce al Tempio near the city walls, where those condemned to death passed their last hours before execution.

The iconographic scheme, which was widely used in the Middle Ages, uses a horizontal rhythm echoed in Jesus' body, the arm of the cross and the city walls, which plays down the dramatic nature of the event.

23

BEATO ANGELICO
Tabernacle
of the Linen-drapers
(Enthroned Virgin
and Child)
(whole and details
of the predella
on the opposite page)

1433

On the doors, outside:
St. Mark and St. Peter
Inside: *St. John the Baptist*
and St. Mark
In the predella:
St. Peter preaches
in the presence of St. Mark,
Adoration of the Magi,
St. Mark's Martyrdom

Panel, 292×176 (closed),
39×56 (each panel
of the predella)
Inv. 1890, no. 879

The large *Tabernacle* commissioned by the Linen-drapers' Guild in 1433 (payment is documented in 1436) was situated in the Residential Room of the Guild in the centre of Florence, demolished at the end of the 19th century. The important public commission demonstrates Fra Angelico's success as a painter at the beginning of the fourth decade of the century. The image of the Madonna recalls the *Majesties* of the previous century and is a perfect harmony of Gothic elegance, strong modelling and clear perspective, like a consciously updated version of them. The figures on the doors are conversing with contemporary sculptors, especially Lorenzo Ghiberti, who received the commission for the marble frame, which was made by two of his assistants.
In the predella the scenes of Jesus and the saints are described with the vivacity of a mystery play in which the city buildings are effective architectural backgrounds.

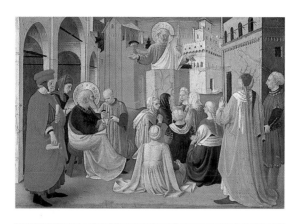

BEATO ANGELICO
San Marco Altarpiece
(Enthroned Virgin and Child, angels, Saints Cosmas, Damian, Lorenzo, John the Evangelist, Mark, Dominic, Francis, Peter the Martyr)
(whole and details of predella on opposite page)

1438-1443

Panel
220×227
Inv. 1890, no. 8506

This Altarpiece, made between 1438 and 1443 for the great altar of the church of San Marco and restored by Michelozzo at the order of Cosimo de' Medici, was to complete and summarize with suitable magnificence the Medicean patronage of San Marco. The painting has been dismantled and was also ruined by a disastrous attempt at cleaning, probably made during the 18th century, which corroded most of the colour especially on the flesh. However it maintains a new appearance of theatricality and large size which make it the real prototype of the Renaissance altarpiece. The circular composition of the *Sacra Conversazione* in a square format, already seen on the *Annalena Altarpiece*, here gains new perspective severity, carefully studied and aided by ingenious inventions such as the fake shrine in the foreground and the geometrical design of the rug, perhaps inspired by one of those donated on the occasion of the 1439 Council. Of the nine predella panels only two remain in San Marco, the others being distributed among museums in Washington, Munich, Dublin and Paris. *The Burial* represents an exceptional document of the architecture of San Marco while the reconstruction of the convent was yet unfinished, following the building of the east-wing dormitory but prior to that above the Hospice looking towards the square and also the dormitory on the north side. In fact, the right arm of the ancient transept has not yet been demolished and can be seen in the background.

The Healing offers a cut-away interior view where the details picked out by the light reveal Fra Angelico's use of painting effects more traditionally favoured by Flemish art.

BEATO ANGELICO
Burial of Cosmas and Damian with their brothers

Predella panel
37×45
Inv. 1890, no. 8494

BEATO ANGELICO
Healing of deacon Justinian

Predella panel
37×45
Inv. 1890, no. 8495

BEATO ANGELICO
Annalena Altarpiece
(Enthroned Virgin and Child,
between Saints Peter the
Martyr, Cosmas, Damian,
John the Evangelist,
Lawrence, Francis)

1434-1435

Panel, 180×202
Inv. 1890, nos. 8493, 8486

The painting came from the monastery of San Vicenzo di Annalena, which no longer exists, and according to a recent theory could originally have been in the church of San Lorenzo. It was commissioned in 1434-5 by Cosimo de' Medici for the family chapel dedicated to Saints Cosmas and Damian. The theory arose due to the presence of various coincidences. The scenes on the predella concern the martyrdom of the two Medicean saints, Cosmas and Damian; in that year Filippo Brunelleschi had insisted that the church altars be decorated with paintings, and the transfer of the *Altarpiece* to the Annalena monastery which was only founded in 1453 might be explained by the modifications to the San Lorenzo chapel in 1461. If this is true it would be the first *Sacra Conversazione* of Renaissance shape and type: with a whole scene contained in a square panel, the figures arranged in a semicircle, it exemplifies of a new concept in painted space.

28

BEATO ANGELICO
Bosco ai Frati Altarpiece
(Enthroned Virgin and Child with Saints Antonio of Padua,Ludovic of Tolosa, Francis, Cosmas, Damian and Peter the Martyr)

after 1450

Panel, 174×174
26×174 (predella)
Inv. 1890
nos. 8503-8507

This was painted for the Franciscan monastery of St.Bonaventure al Bosco ai Frati, in Mugello, restored by Michelozzo and paid for by Cosimo de' Medici straight after the restoration of San Marco. It can be dated after 1450 both due to the presence in the predella of San Bernardino, who was canonised in

that year, and for stylistic reasons. Although it is modelled on the Annalena one, the *Sacra Conversazione* here differs from it in that it has a new awareness of perspective requirements and new dimensions in the architectural background, which certainly bring to mind Roman monuments.

CHAPTERHOUSE

On the opposite side of the cloister is the Chapterhouse, whose external appearance, with exposed stone walls and a doorway flanked by large windows, reveals that it belongs to the 14th century part of the monastery.

Above the door we can still see the sinopite of the fresco depicting St.Dominic holding the Rules and Discipline which allude to the function of the room; here, in keeping with the Rules, the monks' behaviour was discussed and judged.

The fresco, although extensively damaged, has been removed and replaced inside.

The room is dominated by Fra Angelico's large Crucifixion on the end wall, now altered by the missing blue colour of the sky which has been lost over time. The walls are surrounded by walnut wood benches, probably from the 17th century, replacing the original ones.

BEATO ANGELICO
Crucifixion and Saints

1442
Fresco, 550×950

This fresco has a rather unreal appearance, which is also due to the state of repair of the background, originally painted blue and now grey and red, because the pigment has fallen and it can be seen in its preparatory state. As if in a collective reflection on the Crucifixion, historical figures, the founders of the religious orders and the Fathers of the Church appear in the painting: Dominic, Ambrose, Augustine, Benedict, Romuald, Thomas, Jerome, Francis, Bernard, Giovanni Gualberto, Peter the Martyr, as well as Saints linked to the Medici, the monastery and the city: Cosmas, Damian, Law-rence, Mark, John the Baptist. St. Dominic, founder of the Order, is placed under the cross holding up branches of the Dominican family tree which shows the link between the Dominicans and the Crucifix.

**BACCIO
DA MONTELUPO**
Crucifix

1496

Sculpted and painted wood
Height 170
Inv. 1915, no. 278

This large *Crucifix* is in all aspects "natural", both in terms of dimensions and expressivity. It is an assolutely pietistic representation which clearly aims to arouse deep emotions in the observer.

The light runs along the smooth surface which is highly modulated with the anatomical details of a body stretched in physical pain.

The outstanding dramatic effects, like the wound from which blood is flowing and the mouth half-open in exhaustion, highlight the devotional significance impressed on the work by Baccio, an admirer and follower of Savonarola, by whom it was commissioned.

The *Crucifix* is first mentioned in 1496, the year in which Savonarola was prior of San Marco, and was originally situated above the door of the church choir.

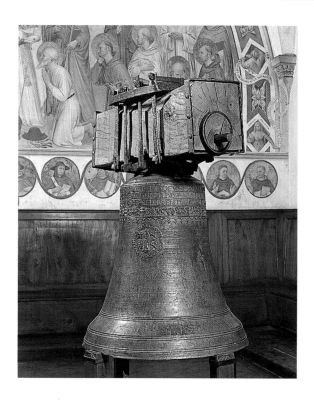

MICHELOZZO (?)
*Bell known
as "la Piagnona"*

c. 1445

Bronze 120×110
Inv. San Marco, no. 348

The bell, better known as *"la Piagnona"*, was originally on the bell-tower of San Marco for which the Medici (whose coat of arms is embossed on the surface) commissioned it on completion of the restoration of the church and monastery,

probably in 1445.
The name *"Piagnona"* derives from the fact that in the 16th century it became the symbol of the anti-Medici faction of Savonarola's Florentine followers; on 8 April 1498 the monastery was attacked in order to capture Savonarola and the bell was rung to call the people to defend the friar. The bell was ignominiously banished to San Salvatore al Monte after the death of Savonarola

and was brought back to San Marco only in 1509.
The frieze of dancing cherubs at the top recalls that of the cathedral choir loft completed by Donatello in 1439 and clearly suggests that it was made in his workshop, perhaps by Michelozzo, who is known to have been a smelter (with varying degrees of success) along with his assistants, including Bartolomeo di Fruosino.

"LAVABO" ROOM

This room, known as the "Lavabo" room due to the ancient function for which it was originally equipped, is also accessible from the cloister and is in front of the Large Refectory, next to the kitchen. Monastery rules imposed the ritual washing and purification of the hands before eating. Above the entrance door is a delicate, but unfortunately damaged, fresco by Fra Angelico depicting Christ in Pietà, *alluding to the Resurrection awaiting those who are nourished by him. Today the room contains works presenting the artistic activity of the second great painter who lived in San Marco at the beginning of the 16th century: Fra Bartolomeo. It also contains works by Luca and Andrea della Robbia whose formal purism constitutes another consequence of Savonarola's influence on art.*

FRA BARTOLOMEO AND MARIOTTO ALBERTINELLI
Last Judgment

1499-1501
Detached fresco
360×375
Inv. 1890, no. 3211

This fresco was ordered in 1499 by an "assistant" in the hospital of Santa Maria Nuova, Gerozzo Dini, for the funeral chapel of his mother Monna Venna in the adjoining Cloister of Bones.

It was left unfinished in 1500 when the painter, influenced by Savonarola, decided to join the Dominican Order and interrupted his artistic activity for at least a year, according to the Rule.

The painting was completed within the first half of 1501 by Mariotto Albertinelli, who had been his companion in the workshop for some years. After a century located in the cemetery the painting's condition had already deteriorated, and this was aggravated by its transfer in 1657 to another cloister after the first was demolished, when it was cut into nine pieces and the figures of the clients were lost. Further damage occurred when it was removed with the wall in 1871. Only a recent and radical "tearing" action of the remaining painted film stopped the crumbling of the colour caused by salts in the *intonaco*. Despite its badly worn condition, the fresco still conveys the extraordinary effect of huge aerial circularity of the composition, which was a source of inspiration for the young Raphael in *Disputation concerning the Sacrament* painted in the Vatican Rooms in 1509. There is a frescoed copy, also from the 16th century, in the church of St. Apollonia and a copy on paper from the end of the 19th century by Raffaello Bonaiuti, now stored in the Florentine Galleries.

LUCA DELLA ROBBIA
Enthroned Virgin and Child
1450-1460
Glazed terracotta
99×47,5×37

This group of unknown origin is mentioned from the 18th century in the oratory of St. Thomas Aquinas where it underwent a ruinous fall at the end of the 19th century and shattered into several pieces. Following its last restoration, after the flood in 1966, it has again become an object of interest. The expressive quality of the modelling confirms the attribution to Luca della Robbia, inventor of the glazed terracotta technique, who here uses a wider colour range than the usual white and blue. Along with the cheerful flash of colour in the Child, this leads us to rethink the early dating suggested and place it nearer in time to works from the sixth decade, like the *Coat of arms of the Guild of Doctors and Chemists* in Orsanmichele or the *Virgin and Child* of Sant'Onofrio at the Bargello.

LARGE REFECTORY

Passing through typically Florentine stone portals from the "Lavabo" room, the visitor can enjoy a splendid perspective view of the adjoining rooms and especially the large space of the Refectory. The room has cross vault ceilings with Medieval style ribs, and partially corresponds to the 14th century room that existed before Michelozzo extended it in order to build the first friars' dormitory above. The last part was annexed in 1529, by extracting it from the hospice and demolishing the end wall of the Refectory on which was painted a Crucifixion by Beato Angelico, which is recalled by sources but has been lost.

Today the Refectory contains a series of paintings from the first half of the 16th century which illustrate the particular devotional tendency of the painters educated by or in contact with the "San Marco School", which began with Fra Bartolomeo at the beginning of the century.

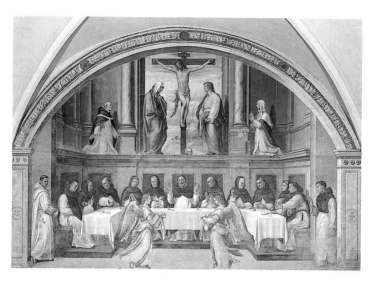

**GIOVANNI ANTONIO
SOGLIANI**
*The miraculous Supper
of St. Dominic*
1536
Fresco, 500×792

The painter's mark and the date 1536 can be seen on the pillars beside the fresco. The iconography uniting the theme of the Crucifixion, common in the 14th century, to that of Providence was obviously chosen by the friars who refused the first subject suggested by the painter, the *Multiplication of the rolls and fishes*, although the preparatory drawings remain.

St. Dominic is shown at the table with his brothers, without food, served by angels, which fulfils the twofold scope of commemorating the founder and inviting the observer to have faith in Providence and Resurrection, symbolised by the Crucifix above. The composition is classicized and the fresco oscillates between the measured realism of the friars' heads and the new lightness of the angels, in Andrea del Sarto's style.

Fra Paolino da Pistoia
*Mystical Marriage
of St. Catherine
and Saints*

c. 1525

Panel
283×218
Inv. 1890, no. 3471

The painting was formerly in the choir of the St. Catherine convent in Cafaggio, located near San Marco for nuns who were followers of Savonarola.

It was inspired by the painting by Fra Bartolomeo today in the Louvre. The painter, also a Dominican friar, would have seen it being painted in the San Marco monastery in 1509. The composition is similar to this

other work but the Saints have been replaced with other members of the Dominican order, or figures particularly revered by it, while other parts of the painting recall works by Fra Bartolomeo. The probable date, around 1525, is suggested by the use of very bright and changing colours which correspond to a precise phase in Fra Paolino's work.

GIOVANNI ANTONIO SOGLIANI
St. Francis
and *St. Elizabeth*
1520-1525

Panel, 218×197
Inv. 1890, nos. 4648, 4649

The two paintings can be dated within the third decade of the 16th century and come from the church of San Girolamo alla Costa in Florence. They are among the most

representative in terms of type and quality of this painter's work.

The austere and realistic painting offering effective hints of realism, like the crown at the feet of St. Elizabeth, reveals expert drawing and refined taste, as well as the full adhesion to the main Savonarola artists of the "San Marco School", characterised by simplicity and pathos.

FRA BARTOLOMEO ROOM

This room occupies the former kitchen of the monastery, where all the service rooms are located around a little Cloister known as the "Spesa". Today it contains an exhibition of paintings by Fra Bartolomeo; the painter was a follower of Savonarola and took the Dominican habit in 1500. He kept a painting studio in San Marco until his death in 1517. Basing his work on the preliminaries of rational 15th century classicism, Fra Bartolomeo developed a style of art which was freer in its use of colour space and design and inspired the young Raphael.

FRA BARTOLOMEO
Ecce Homo

1501-1502

Fresco on flat tile, 51,5×37
Inv. 1890, no. 8520

This may be the oldest of the frescoes on tile painted for the Caldine monastery and transferred to San Marco in the 18th century. Its formal and conceptual purism corresponds to the radiant image of Christ which Savonarola sketched in the *Triumph of the Cross* (1492).

FRA BARTOLOMEO
St. Mary Magdalene

c. 1506

Fresco on flat tile, 47×35
Inv. 1890, no. 8512

This was painted for the friar's private worship, perhaps originally on the wall of the Mary Magdalene monastery. The painting records the painter's love of light effects and transparence, permitted by the fresco technique, which were typical of his style at the turn of the century.

FRA BARTOLOMEO
Signoria Altarpiece
(Virgin and Child, St. Anne
and other Saints)

1510-1513
Panel
444×305
Inv. 1890, no. 1574

The painting is still in its preparatory state, the stage after the brush drawing from the cartoon, in which the figures have been shaded to give an idea of their dimensions before colouring.

It is known as the *Signoria Altarpiece* because it was commissioned in 1510 by Pier Soderini, "gonfaloniere" of the Republic, for the new Council Room in Palazzo Vecchio, where Parliament met in 1494. The theme is a *Sacra Conversazione* between the Patron Saints of Florence about the Immaculate Conception, a conversation which symbolised free democratic discussion.

When the Republic fell in 1513, and the historical-political significance of the painting faded, the *Altarpiece* was left unfinished. Since then it was moved around a great deal until its return to San Marco this century.

FRA BARTOLOMEO
Portrait of Savonarola

1498-1499 c.
Panel, 46,5×32,5
Inv. 1890, no. 8550

This is the first of two portraits painted by Fra Bartolomeo, admirer and loyal follower of Savonarola, just after the monk was tortured in 1498. The portrait came into the possession of Sister Caterina de' Ricci, a fervent follower of Savonarola, along with some other belongings, and purchased by the museum only in the twentieth century. The influence of Flemish painting can be glimpsed in the light used to realistically model the planes of the face.

FRA BARTOLOMEO
Portrait of Girolamo Savonarola as St. Peter the Martyr

1508-1510
Panel, 52×40
Inv. 1890, no. 8522

A few years after the first portrait Fra Bartolomeo painted another, destined for the Caldine monastery (now on display in the Savonarola Chapel on the first floor) in which the monk is depicted as St. Peter the Martyr.
The double intention here was both to glorify the figure of Savonarola and conceal his identity, so as to be able to spread his image at a time when any commemoration or worship of Savonarola was prohibited.

"Spesa" Cloister

This little cloister is part of Michelozzo's reconstruction carried out around 1440, except for the little arcade, built in the 17ᵗʰ century, which is to be found on the upper floor covering the original terrace and perhaps intended as a clothes drying area for the monastery.

The cloister backs onto the east perimeter wall, on via La Pira, and its dimensions and type recall the Lodge in the Annunciation *frescoed by Beato Angelico at the top of the stairs leading to the Dormitory.*

Its function was to link the service wing to the Lodge and the ground floor to the first floor, because in the corner of one of its sides was the spiral staircase formerly joining the two floors, before it was demolished and replaced possibly in the 17ᵗʰ century by the staircase which still exists today. This leads to the underground rooms, location of the lapidarium along with part of the collection of tombstones from the old centre of Florence, the Granary, the vestibule of the Lodge and the Small Refectory. It can be visited in summer.

STANDARD ROOM

This room is opposite the former kitchen and was certainly used for service functions connected with it, as shown by the presence of a stone sink found in the wall during the last restoration work, and of a link with the underground area, then used as a cellar, and with a mezzanine. Today it contains a large standard from the mid-15th century, formerly attributed to Baldovinetti after whom the room was named, around which are collected 15th century paintings by artists influenced by Beato Angelico, some of whom were from outside Florence.

FRANCESCO BOTTICINI
Sant'Antonino
worships the Crucifix
(left)
c. 1460
Canvas
276×147
Inv. San Marco, no. 277

The canvas is painted with a thin layer of paint with little binder and hardly any preparation, as was usual for a standard (which is what this was) according to sour-ces. It has been ruino-usly restored and un-fortunately extensive-ly damaged, but is still legible.

The original rectangu-lar shape, which can be seen at the top, was later changed into an arch shape and the canvas was thus fitted into the enormous, late 15th cen-tury frame it occupies today. The picture was painted after the death in 1459 of Antonino Pierozzi, prior of the monastery and bishop of Florence, and shows quite strongly the in-fluence of Andrea del Castagno in the nervous outlining and the in-sistence on anatomical detail. Formerly attrib-uted to Alesso Baldo-vinetti, it is now agreed that Francesco Botticini is the artist although a document states it was painted in 1483 by Pol-laiolo.

BENOZZO GOZZOLI
Mystical Marriage of
St. Catherine (detail below),
Christ in the tomb with
St. John and Mary Mag-
dalene, St. Anthony Ab-
bot and St. Benedict
c. 1460
Panel
21×221
Inv. 1890, no. 886

The painter of the Al-tarpiece which this pre-della accompanied is unknown, but the pre-della itself comes from the church of Santa Cro-ce, whence it was taken to the Florentine Gal-leries in 1847.

It is similar in style to the 1459 frescoes in the Magi Chapel in Palazzo Medici, and is a mature work by this artist.

Here the influence of Fra Angelico, whose pupil he had been for twenty years, is only one element of his style, which is more descrip-tive and modelled than the Master's.

FIRST FLOOR DORMITORIES

On the upper floor, made by Michelozzo between 1437 and 1446 by raising the existing medieval rooms, are the friars' dormitories. They consist of three corridors surrounding the cloister on three sides, which is overlooked by the 43 cells frescoed by Beato Angelico between 1438 and 1443.

Today it can be reached by a staircase, perhaps built in the 17th century replacing the original spiral staircase (placed in a different location) which led directly in front of the fresco of the Annunciation. *This is one of the three frescoes painted outside the cells by Fra Angelico (along with* St. Dominic worships the Crucifix *and the* Sacra Conversazione *known as* Virgin of the Shadows*) before which the friars recited a common prayer at the times and in the ways prescribed by the Dominican Rule.*

In each cell is a fresco concerning the Life and Passion of Christ, *for the exclusive contemplation of the friar occupying the cell.*

Savonarola's cells were not frescoed because they originally held clothing. Some of the cells were demolished in the 17th century to create the vestibule in front of the library.

This cycle of frescoes, unique in the world, is considered to be completely the work of Fra Angelico, although he was helped by assistants including Benozzo Gozzoli; the overall project for the decoration and sinopite of all the frescoes was definitely the Master's.

BEATO ANGELICO
Annunciation
(whole and details
next page)

c. 1440
Fresco
230×297

This is one of the most famous images of Renaissance art, as well as one of Fra Angelico's and San Marco's most well known work, and its symbolic image. The three novelties of the new age are contained in it: Fra Angelico's light painting, the clarity of Florentine architecture and spatial and perspective severity.

The scene is set under a bare arcade, simply plastered, with round arches and classical partly Corinthian and partly Ionic capitals, which recalls the arcade of the cloister just built by Michelozzo on the ground floor of the monastery. This would suggest that it can be dated within 1443 near the time of their construction. There are no decorative elements or collateral episodes like the *Flight from Eden* which are usually included in representations of this subject in panel paintings, even previous ones by Fra Angelico himself. The painter clearly wished to concentrate totally on the intimacy and spirituality of the situation.

FIRST CORRIDOR CELLS

To the left of the Annunciation *is the Fathers' Corridor, the first built by Michelozzo to house the Dominican friars who had just settled into the monastery, which was left in an unliveable state by the Sylvestrians (according to monastery records) and in conditions of extreme neglect.*
In 1437 the first twenty cells had already been completed, arranged on both sides of the corridor and soon after were frescoed by Beato Angelico, each with a scene from the Life of Christ.
On the left side are ten cells which were all painted by Fra Angelico while those on the right were designed by the Master but often painted by faithful assistants.

Cell 1
BEATO ANGELICO
"Noli me tangere"

1438-1443
Fresco
166×125

The fresco uses a very limited colour range and is an extraordinary example of Fra Angelico's new style of art. The style was new in its compositional concept which made the landscape as much a protagonist in the picture as the figures, due to the use of light as a vehicle for real and unreal representation, and the severe sense of space despite certain incongruities in the figures like that of Christ depicted appearing to Mary Magdalene as a gardener, with his feet in a most improbable position.

Cell 2
BEATO ANGELICO
Lamentation over Christ deposed from the Cross

1438-1443

Fresco
184×152

The figure of St. Dominic appears for the first time in this scene, and will constantly appear in all the others as a symbolic witness of the holy events. The iconographic model is the same one used by the painter in this period for the painting in the church of Santa Maria della Croce al Tempio, now displayed in the Hospice.

The more measured rhythm of the figures, the bare setting and delicate colour range in the fresco produce a much more spiritual effect than the panel.

Cell 3
BEATO ANGELICO
Annunciation

1438-1443
Fresco
176×148

This scene was intended for private contemplation and has lost even the slightest reference to the setting which it had in the large version at the top of the stairs. Here the painter has concentrated on portraying the silent dialogue laden with significance, a dialogue attended by St. Peter of Verona (one of the Dominican protomartyrs) who can be see on the left, if only in the imagination.

The architecture with its severe perspective seems to be simply a pretext to continue reproducing into the background the arch traced by the figures in the foreground .

Cell 6
BEATO ANGELICO
Transfiguration

1505-1506
Fresco
181×152

In this fresco the chromatic and compositional quality of Fra Angelico's art reach their peak.

The scene represents the greatest possible synthesis of abstraction and solidity.

The spatial setting is absolutely realistic in the circle traced by the figures called to witness the scene – the Virgin, St. Peter, St. James, St. John, St. Dominic, Elias and Moses – around the figure of Christ.

The overall effect is a visionary image with Christ as the focal point, a living image of the Cross, paled with light, engulfing and transfiguring also those present.

53

Cell 7
BEATO ANGELICO
The Mocking of Christ

1438-1443
Fresco
187×151

Within the extremely austere perspective frame, the grieving Virgin and young St. Dominic deep in prayer introduce a meditation of the blindfolded Christ, depicted enthroned behind them holding the cane and the globe; these are symbols of the power offered him in contempt by his tormentors.

On the unrealistic green background, the various symbols of mockery traditionally portrayed in Medieval symbolism surround the Christ figure: hands slapping him and striking him and faces spitting on him.

Corridor
BEATO ANGELICO
Virgin of the Shadows
(whole and detail)

c. 1443

Fresco and tempera
193×273, 130×273 "balza"
(perspective floor)

This fresco is known as *Virgin of the Shadows* due to the shadows created by the leaves on the capitals invested with natural light from the window. It is in reality a "Sacra Conversazione" which includes all the Patron Saints of the monastery and its occupants. These Saints are: Dominic, Cosmas, Damian, Mark, John the Evangelist, Thomas, Law-rence and Peter the Martyr. It was painted in tempera on a fresco base and its materials and composition recall the altarpieces Fra Angelico was painting in that period.

There are two schools of thought concerning the dating of this fresco, which is still uncertain: the first, shared by this writer, is that it was the last of all the frescoes to be painted, by the end of 1443, while the other dates it later, on the artist's return from Rome after 1450, due to the compositional maturity and the grandeur of the architectural background.

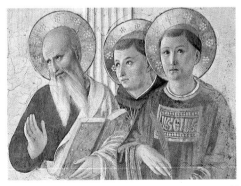

Cell 8
BEATO ANGELICO
The Marias
at the Tomb

1438-1443
Fresco
181×151

With its subject material concentrated in the narrow cave, the fresco is conceptually organised as an extended play of mental references. The vision of the whole scene is conceived by St. Dominic, who is beautifully portrayed in the left corner, while the vision of Christ resurrected is in the mind of the Virgin Mary, surprised by the discovery.

The chromatic expertise in the graduation between the passages and in the elegance of the comparisons produces an entirely harmonious overall effect.

Cell 10
BEATO ANGELICO
Presentation
in the Temple

1438-1443
Fresco
171×116

Thanks to the recovery, during recent restoration, of the niche with shell-valve semi-dome, previously hidden behind red repainting, the fresco has regained its original harmonious relationship between figures and setting, under the fundamental action of the light altering the colours of the priest's vestments. St. Peter the Martyr can be seen on the left. The female figure on the right is difficult to identify; she may be somehow connected to him or alternatively may simply be a protagonist in the scene.

Novices' Corridor

This dormitory was reserved for novices and only contains seven cells which open onto the interior side of the cloister; there are also three rooms at the top of the corridor known as Savonarola's cells. Thanks to the recent discovery of wall painting on the perimeter walls under the floor, it can be dated between the end of the 13th century and the beginning of the 14th. It can also now be seen that the current floor was at roof level. The cells are all the same, larger than those of the fathers, each one frescoed with St. Dominic worshipping the Crucifix, attributed to Benozzo Gozzoli. In the last two cells before Savonarola's, some of the friar's belongings are displayed like the processional standard, cloak and small devotional cross.

CIRCLE OF FRANCESCO BOTTICINI (MASTER OF THE FIESOLE EPIPHANY?)

Processional standard with Crucifix
(front side)
c. 1490
Tempera painted on linen
103×65
Inv. 1915, no. 494

This is an extremely rare painting with regard to history and type. On both sides of the processional standard is the image of the Crucifix traditionally attributed to Fra Angelico and belonging to Savonarola, and usually carried by him in processions. Recent restoration work has made the light painting of the outlines more legible and confirmed that it does not belong to the corpus of Fra Angelico's work which was already agreed on in the 19th century; the suggested dating is towards the end of the 15th century.

This period corresponds to the time Savonarola spent in San Marco and the painting is attributed to Francesco Botticini's circle, in which artists in close contact with Savonarola's set were working, like the anonymous Master of the Fiesole Epiphany who may be the author of this work.

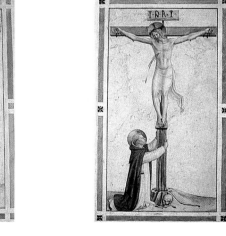

Cells 20, 16, 17, 15
BEATO ANGELICO
AND BENOZZO GOZZOLI
St. Dominic worships
the Crucifix

1440-1443
Frescoes
103×172

The frescoes in the Novices' Corridor cells all depict St. Dominic worshipping the Crucifix in different attitudes, from imploration to self-flagellation. The didactic function of this type of iconography was to portray St. Dominic's pre-

cepts regarding the method of prayer as indicated by him.
The images recall the similar ones by Fra Angelico, but the more insistent and descriptive drawing and painting suggest the work of the young Benozzo Gozzoli.

SAVONAROLA'S CELLS

At the end of the Novices' Corridor are three rooms which were used by Fra Girolamo Savonarola as oratory, study and cell. The oratory was transformed and embellished in 1701 when the monks decided to display there the works of Fra Bartolomeo that they still possessed and which are now displayed in the ground floor room dedicated to the painter. On that occasion the commission was given to Alessandro Gherardini to paint the oval fresco on the ceiling with the Glory of St. Catherine, *removed in the 19th century and now placed above the entrance door. Many works came from the Dominican monastery of St. Mary Magdalene at Caldine, including the rectangular fresco, detached with a section of wall, of the* Virgin and Child, *now on the right wall. During the building of the Museum in the 19th century, when an attempt was made to put to fruitful use the rooms connected with the figure of Savonarola, two other detached frescoes were placed there: the* Christ the Pilgrim *from the "Spesa" Cloister in San Marco and the arched* Virgin and Child *from the Magdalene monastery at Caldine. Just after the inauguration of the Museum the chapel contained the* Monument to Girolamo Savonarola *sculpted in 1873 by Giovanni Dupré while in the study and cell were a collection of objects belonging to him.*

FRA BARTOLOMEO
Virgin and Child

1514

Detached fresco
120×78

The fresco was transferred from the Magdalene monastery in 1867 and can be identified as one of the two recorded as being painted in 1514, i.e. the one at the foot of the stairs. There are various copies on panel of this painting: the turning of the figures, the spiral composition and the light drawing, are influenced by Raphael Sanzio; Fra Bartolomeo had become familiar with Raphael's work during the painter's Florentine period between 1504 and 1508 and his Roman journey in 1513-1514.

In this work the echo of the *Madonna della Seggiola* (1514, now in Palazzo Pitti) is particularly evident.

GIOVANNI DUPRÉ
Monument to
Girolamo Savonarola
1873
Marble and bronze
246×175×45 (marble);
57×61×55 (bronze)

This academic-style sculpture consists of a bust portrait placed on a marble sarcophagus with three episodes from the life of Savonarola in relief.

On the front is the *Proposal of the Republic Statutes to the "Gonfalonieri"*, on the sides *Vocation* and *Sacrifice*. This was the expression of a catholic movement during the "rediscovery" of the monk which took place in the 19th century by opposing factions.

61

**FLORENTINE PAINTER
END OF 15TH CENTURY**
*Martyrdom of
Savonarola in Piazza
della Signoria*
c. 1498
Panel
101×117
Inv. San Marco, no. 477

There are many copies of this panel which illustrates the execution of Fra Girolamo and two of his supporters in Piazza della Signoria on 23 May 1498, and the events immediately before this, like his presentation before the Tribunal on the railings of Palazzo Vecchio and his divestiture. The episode described is not however the true protagonist of the painting, which is dominated by the view of the Piazza and surrounding city. This is confirmed by the absence of participation in the event on the part of members of the public, who are walking around the square talking, with total indifference to what is taking place. The accurate representation of the churches and buildings, the view from above and the similarity to the engraved Catena Map lead us to think that it has the same author, Francesco Rosselli, illuminator and engraver of geographical maps.

FIRST CORRIDOR CELLS

Cell 22
**BEATO ANGELICO
AND BENOZZO GOZZOLI**
*Crucifix and
the mourning Virgin*

1438-1443
Fresco
144×81

Similar to the one on the Novices' Cells, it only differs in the presentation of the figure of the Virgin Mary in-

stead of St. Dominic. The painting is characterised by an elaborate style, and seems more in accordance with the work of Benozzo Gozzoli. However the plastic and spatial definition of the Virgin betrays the direct hand of the Master.

Under the floor of the cell fragments of frescoes were found a few

years ago which were dated at the second half of the 14th century, leading the walls to be dated at the time of the Sylvestrians, the first residents of the monastery.

One of these is a lunette above an arch with the *Vir dolorum between St. Benedict and another Saint*, and another shows a geometric design on a fake fabric.

Cell 24
BEATO ANGELICO
AND ASSISTANTS
Baptism of Christ

1438-1443
Fresco
179×148

This is one of the few frescoes on this side of the first corridor which shows a different subject from the *Crucifixion*.

In this scene the landscape dominates uncontested over the figures, with a pearly colour-scheme creating a surreal effect.

Thus while the idea of the river trailing into the horizon among the desert-like rocks cannot fail to recall the inventiveness of Beato Angelico, the slight figures, like cutout silhouettes, go beyond corporeal naturalness and Angelical expressivity.

They announce, in formal simplicity, the work of one or more assistants to the Master.

THIRD CORRIDOR CELLS

The cells of the third corridor, reserved for clerics and guests, include two cells reserved for Cosimo de' Medici, where pope Eugenio IV slept the night of Epiphany 1443 when he came to consecrate the new church. The frescoes in these cells have rather different features to the others. The repertoire is wider and even the Crucifixions *have various schemes and variations. The language is more descriptive and the colours are brighter, the composition is more complex and next to the Master the contribution of assistants increases, including Benozzo Gozzoli.*
When the window to the cloister was opened in the 17th century two cells were partially demolished along with two frescoes – the Temptation of Christ in the desert *and the* Triumphant Entrance to Jerusalem.

Cell 35
BEATO ANGELICO
AND ASSISTANTS
*The Institution
of the Eucharist*

1459-1443
Fresco
186×254

Although largely painted by the Master's assistants (evident from the rather repetitive textual schemes), this fresco is very interesting thanks to the architectural setting which is similar to San Marco. The idea of describing the view of the opposite wing of the building through the mullioned windows is ingenious, as it makes the scene appear to take place inside a cell from which there really is such a view. To the right of the fresco the glimpse of the well is a fine example of "verismo" which calls to mind Flemish-style works.

Cell 31
**BEATO ANGELICO
AND ASSISTANTS**
Christ in Limbo

1439-1443
Fresco
183×166

Cell 31 is traditionally supposed to have been Sant'Antonino's, prior of the monastery from 1439 before being appointed bishop of Florence in 1446.

When the Museum was created in the 19th century the cell was embellished with objects linked to the saint's life, including his family tree, his plaster death mask and other valuable manuscripts occasionally displayed today in the Library.

The scene is rich in descriptive detail which makes it one of the most vivid frescoes here. Its luminosity is still totally the work of Beato Angelico although an assistant seems to have painted the figures in the background.

Cell 39
BEATO ANGELICO
AND BENOZZO GOZZOLI
*Adoration
of the Magi*
(whole and detail)

1440-1443

Fresco
175×357;
86×60 (tabernacle)

Cells 38 and 39 were the rooms Cosimo de' Medici reserved for periods of spiritual retreat in the monastery, and pope Eugenio IV also stayed here when he came to San Marco for Epiphany 1443, to consecrate the restored church.

The purpose of Cell 38 is evident from the presence of St. Cosmas among the onlookers at the *Crucifixion* which is stylistically attributable to Gozzoli like the rest of the painting, and by the background painted with azurite, an expensive pigment which was not used in the other cells, probably in honour of the Rule of poverty.

In Cell 39, on the other hand, is the *Adoration of the Magi*, still in its preparatory state; during the latest restoration incongruous additions in the form of bushes on the ground, clouds in the sky and blue repainting of the Virgin's cloak, were removed.

The compositional, chromatic and formal characteristics of this high quality fresco are typical of Fra Angelico, and the forms and typology record his impressions of the Council held in Florence in 1439.

Cell 42
BEATO ANGELICO
Crucifixion with
St. Mark, St. Dominic,
Longino, Martha and
Mary

1440-1443
Fresco
196×199

This is one of the most successful compositions of this cycle thanks to the design and articulation of the figures within the space, although it also one of the least known.

The artist reaches a peak of expressivity and chromatic intensity in his portrayal of the women's grief, and these figures recall the similar ones in the large *Crucifixion* in the Chapterhouse.

The extension of the figures over the space, the measured rhythm, and the solidity of the bodies express the painter's full artistic maturity and suggest that this and the other frescoes on this side of the corridor, are dated later, just before completion of the whole work.

LIBRARY

Stripped of the pluteuses with which it was originally furnished and the wall cupboards which replaced them in the 17th century, the Library's bare architecture is revealed, highlighting its basilical structure with three naves, flanked by stone columns and classical ionic capitals. It was conceived as a real temple of knowledge and contrasts sharply with the simplicity of the other rooms. Cosimo de' Medici took care to provide the necessary volumes and also commissioned a series of liturgical books to Zanobi Strozzi, a pupil of Beato Angelico. This was the first Renaissance library to be opened to the public and was ordered by Vespasiano da Bisticci according to the dictates of Tommaso da Sarzana, who later became pope Niccolò V. It was later enriched by the book collection belonging to the humanist Niccolò Niccoli, which included many Greek texts.

BEATO ANGELICO
Virgin Patron
of the Dominicans
Ms. 558, initial S at c. 41v.

c. 1425

Illuminated parchment

The *Missal* was probably illuminated by Fra Angelico, while he was in the Fiesole monastery before coming to San Marco, and others, including perhaps the young Zanobi Strozzi. His wealth of miniatures, which is a real gallery of Angelican painting, closely correspond to the early panel paintings such as the *Polyptych* in San Domenico at Fiesole, work of the young Beato Angelico. The *Missal* shows the sophisticated calligraphy of late Gothic taste and the lively colours of the period.

ZANOBI STROZZI
AND FILIPPO DI MATTEO
TORELLI
Ascension
of Mary Magdalene
Ms. 514, initial D at c. 3r

1446-1454

Illuminated parchment

The *Gradual* is one of eleven choir-books illuminated by the two artists, commissioned by Cosimo de' Medici, for the monastery of San Marco.
Zanobi drew the letters and Filippo the decorative plants, while the calligrapher was Fra Benedetto, brother of Fra Angelico.

SMALL REFECTORY

After visiting the upper floors, we return to the ground floor by the same stair-case and to the right enter a small room once used as a refectory for monastery guests staying in the adjoining guest Lodge. It may also have been used as the refectory for sick monks being treated in the infirmary, from the 17th century situated inside the Lodge.

It was decorated by Ghirlandaio only about fifty years after the construction of the monastery and today contains some glazed terracotta relief works from the Della Robbia studio, dated a little later than the Last Supper.

DOMENICO GHIRLANDAIO
Last Supper
(whole and detail
next page)
1479-1480
Fresco
420×780

Considered to be the twin of the one in Ognissanti, it is one of four Last Suppers painted by Ghirlandaio over a five-year period. This seems to be earlier than the one in Ognissanti, painted in 1480, in which the compositional concept, also expressed here, evolves dynamically in the dialogue between the apostles. Like the other frescoes, the composition adapts to the space available. The table and benches arranged in a "U" and the arcade in the background, positioned in accordance with precepts of perspective, attempt to increase by illusion the depth of the room, which is quite limited. Recent restoration work has brought to light the diffuse luminosity of the interior and exterior of the scene, where the real garden and the symbolic garden, in keeping with tastes of that period, actually come together.

ANDREA DELLA ROBBIA
Deposition from the Cross

1505-1510
Glazed terracotta
245×188

This beautiful relief work portrays the Virgin, St. John and Mary Magdalene lamenting the body of Jesus just deposed from the Cross. Unfortunately it is quite ruined due to prolonged exposure outside: it was actually situated in a shrine (now demolished) near Calenzano. Its original purpose is revealed by the engraving under the relief which invites the traveller to pause for a moment to reflect and pray. The portrayal of such expressive intensity and strongly devotional tone was favoured by Andrea della Robbia's workshop at the end of the 15th century, in observance of the exhortations regarding the educational nature of art voiced by Girolamo Savonarola, of whom the Della Robbia brothers were fervent admirers and followers.

FORMER LODGE

Beyond the vestibule linking the St. Dominic Cloister, now property of the Dominican friars, to the small Cloister known as the "Spesa", is a large barrel vaulted gallery which once faced onto the extensive monastery vegetable gardens and where a small garden is situated today which leads to the Museum exit.

A series of small rooms opens onto the gallery, their entrance doors decorated by Fra Bartolomeo with five lunettes depicting Dominican Saints – St. Vincenzo Ferreri, St. Peter the Martyr, the blessed Ambrogio Sansedoni, St. Dominic and St. Thomas – who seem to be the painter's holy brothers in disguise.

These rooms, originally destined for use as a lodge – a place of welcome for passing travellers and, at least from the 17th century, an infirmary – have since the end of the 19th century contained a particular section of the Museum dedicated to stone and pictorial discoveries rescued from the late 19th century demolitions in the Old Centre of Florence. Some of these survived the total destruction of the Ghetto, an area considered irrecoverable from a hygienic-sanitary point of view.

The findings are still arranged according to type using a didactic system adopted by the curator of that period, who takes credit for their preservation: Guido Carocci.

FRA BARTOLOMEO
St. Dominic

1511-1512
Fresco
74×120

This is one of five effigies of the Saints and blessed of the Order, painted by Fra Bartolomeo over some of the doors of rooms in the lodge, and three were added in the 18th century by a painter still unknown.

The images were certainly inspired by those painted by Fra Angelico in the Sant'Antonino Cloister but differ from them in the great expressive power of the faces – real portraits of the holy brothers – and the strength of gesture and gaze.

The technique reveals strongly shaded painting, with rapid brushstrokes, and is contemporary with the *Signoria Altarpiece*.

UNKNOWN FLORENTINE PAINTER
Fragment of wall painting

14th century
Detached fresco, 107×107
Inv. 1925, no. 250

The fragment came from the Lamberti house in via Pellicceria. An illusionistic wall decoration, rich in strongly naturalistic plant and animal elements, it was rescued, like others, from the demolition of public and private buildings.

ANDREA DI NOFRI
Portal

1414-1433
"Pietra serena", 463×329×40
Inv. 1925, no. 47

This beautiful portal dated between 1414 and 1433 comes from the headquarters of the Guild of Second-hand dealers, Linen-drapers and Tailors in Piazza Sant'Andrea. From the same building came the large *Tabernacle* painted by Fra Angelico, completed in 1433. Together with the other one preserved here, from the Guild of Hoteliers, it provides a fairly detailed idea of the majestic dimensions and severe appearance of the Guild buildings. On the lintel are the shields of the Second-hand dealers, the People's Captain, the Florentine Church, the Republic of Florence and the Guelph party, on a background dominated by Anjou lilies.

SYLVESTRIAN CLOISTER

From one of the rooms in the Lodge, containing the display of stone find-
ings from the Old Centre, it is possible to visit – in spring and summer – a
small cloister with cross vaulted gallery, part of the original construction
built by the Sylvestrian monks.

Its 14th century construction is indicated by columns and pillars with leaf
capitals. Under the vaulting today the tablets and family arms of the San
Pancrazio Church burial ground (one of the oldest ecclesiastical build-
ings in the city, now the Marini Museum) removed during the late 19th cen-
tury, are displayed in chronological order.

Among the most interesting works are a paleo-Christian tablet reused in
the 14th century and an elegant monument from the end of the 15th century
to abbot Vincenzo Trinci. The burial area is of historical as well as artis-
tic interest thanks to the glimpse it offers us of the social structure of this
area of the city; aristocratic coats-of-arms can be seen alongside those of
ordinary citizens identified by their craft or business.

In the adjoining courtyard, known as the Granary due to its former use as
a grain storehouse, portals and columns can still be seen, which also came
from the demolition of the historical buildings which include the Portal of
the Pazzi gardens.

INDEX

Printed in June 1999
at Giunti Industrie Grafiche S.p.A. – Prato